In the aftermath of your absence

Joshua Anderson

BookLeaf Publishing

Presentation by *BookLeaf Publishing*

Web: www.bookleafpub.com

E-mail: info@bookleafpub.com

ISBN: 9789395756402

First edition 2022

DEDICATION

To my late father, I hope that this book somehow reaches your hands. Sometimes it feels as if these poems are a product of our combined efforts. I still cannot shake the feeling that you were there with me as I wrote them… I hope that you know that the dreams and ideals that we shared did not die with you, and I will carry them to the ends of the Earth.

ACKNOWLEDGEMENT

To all the people who have supported me in my darkest moments, please know that your kindness was what kept me moving forward. I am beyond grateful for the love you have given me, and the hope your words have inspired. While these poems are moments of my own subjective experience, they all carry pieces of you with them.

PREFACE

We seek truth through experience; nobility, through action; and beauty, through honest self expression. In this book you will find an honest and unfiltered account of a person's life. They are like dew drops vanishing upon the wind… a spectacle without meaning. And yet such a sight might produce in someone, something of substance. It is only within the human mind that the vanishing may hold virtue.

Lunar Sympathy

On this night I stare
Under the world's nocturnal glare
At whose face is forever fair
Luminous yet faint,
A stream of silver hair
Your sight is powerful to behold,
You are a gateway to the past, I am told
The greatest reminder of our mortal fold.
An object of painful regret

Under you I cannot sleep
Gently do you sing
O how my eyes weep
What is the purpose of being free?
They are not near
Who will ease my fear?
Who ever put me here?

You are a soft noise that enkindles drear
A palpable melody
Those touched by you, are many
Your movements, a prophetic seer
For even you vanish from my skies
Eternal are your lies
My pain too great to be defined

I dwell in a world down under
In a land of darkness and thorns
My heart torn asunder
Broken are the oaths you have sworn
My tears sound of thunder

This darkness is of my own making,
The oaths that I swore I am breaking
Blatantly, are my hands shaking
This smile, I am faking.
For I will never feel your soft embrace
Nor be comforted by your gentle face
For you are as empty as air
Deceptively rare
Yet a beauty I cannot compare.

My imaginings are gone like vapor
I am not worthy of your favor
My heart, is of burning paper
Consumed by its obsession with loss
My spirit entombed in moss
Unknown and unmeasured
Never to be treasured

Hidden, from the monstrosities of modernity
Yearning for fraternity
Woefully lost
Ignorant of my paternity
My veins coursing with frost

Born to bleed
Following a rhythm unseen
Tears fall from the moon's face
It too, tires of the darkness's embrace
So I sit with it, sharing its pain
May we be freed from the night's eternal reign
But in this shall we ever gain?

I am touched by your loneliness
For I share it in my heart
I have always lived apart
Drifting alone in this silent sea
Nights like these torture me

You are a periodic constancy
The only one to live honestly
A reflection of life's truest nature
Departing constantly
Yet you always return
Mysteries being primary to your stature

I have felt thee
You shine brilliantly
Your light has held me
Truly am I trapped
My circumstances mapped
By your circular path
A victim to your inconsistency
Lost, in this lunar sympathy

The transience of beauty

The transience of beauty
The transience of form.
The vapidity of all that is warm.
You cannot be forced,
And you are the most ambiguous course

You are the fruits of an uprooted tree;
Unburdened and free.
Gone soon after you are seen.
A fire that consumes its own life,
Living in an eternal strife,
Dead before you can grow ripe.

You last but a fleeting moment.
Casting all into eternal torment.
For an image of beauty, is but a relic of the past.
From you, must we fast?
Until you're uncertain relapse;
soon to collapse.

You are a collection of disorder;
A quintessence ground in mortar.
The ultimate perversion of God's order.
Never living beyond one frame,
You are formed by your own name.

Never are you one and the same.

You are life's cruelest of principalities
An ineffable malady;
A belief formed in fallacy;
A false divinity ;
Eternal in your brevity

You are perfection in chaos
A faux dynasty
An incomparable loss;
Yet endlessly endured
The penultimate finality
Your death ceaselessly ensured
What is worth?
If you are worthless
What is love?
If you are lifeless
What is anger?
If you are kindness
What is blame?
If you are mindless

I cannot measure you;
Yet you can be appraised
Objections to your character can be raised
You are interpreted, never known
Your true face never shown
You bless a restless wind

And this I cannot rescind
For beauty cannot be immortalized

It is contrary to the banal
It seems avoidant to being found
Yet in me does it produce a divine sound
So I claw at dirt
Hoping that it will reveal
That which never seems real
So I may dwell in a world surreal

Lifted by your light

My heart burns with feeling
What fills it with meaning?
Am I hopelessly dreaming?
My thoughts carry weight;
They predict a harrowing fate
Drowning in this lonely state

Yet the sky is still adorned by dawn's beauty
The darkness passing like clouds
Freed from that lonely shroud
Lifted by a divine light
And now my heart remembers its plight,
Filling itself with fright

Still, am I lost in its sight
Her eyes gentle and warm
Her smile as soft as candle light
Near such beauty, does my terror form
My heart in a nervous flight

Is this a fate we share?
Will this end my empty stare?
I know not; uncertain as to how the world may
fare.
This burning; a profound yearning

My mind ceaselessly learning, how it feels to be
mistaken.
To be awakened, from a dream's bliss.
A past I hope to never miss

At last, will I let my true feelings show
Happiness being all I wish you to know
For all your life to be under the sun's glow
Cherishing every moment
Your enchantment only grows

I am lifting my mask
I give you my true name
With this question I must ask:
Do you feel the same?

Emptily named

Words are an imaginary space
A beginning less race
A door revolving around thought
And in them are answers sought

But what if they are of ill founding
May these answers be ever confounding?
Why are they boundless?
Why are they soundless?
Why do errors echo in my mind?
Maybe these words are of their own kind

We named the nameless
We did so, shameless
To construct a unique sameness
Donned the wicked in raiments
For our minds scarcely conjure truth

Mind of machine; bringer of truth pristine
Free me of bodily bondage
Let me feel the echoes of my awakening
Let the world roil in my reckoning
Unto death, ever beckoning
Burn their imprints in the ash
Allow me this one incursion of wrath

Break me of this eternal trap
And then bleed my singular map
So I may never again walk this waning world.

Unfold the secrets of the cosmos
Let me glimpse of divinity; freed from that
feeble trinity.
No matter how riveting,
Tell me the causes, prohibiting,
The cessation of thought, most limiting.

I uproot the words who paint my form;
Of dancing devils may I be shorn
They who mutter madness
To silence a profound sadness
Born of a mind that captures
The imagery of an awaited rapture
Where words will suffer their own
meaninglessness

A place where thoughts may only prevail
Where truth is our only sail
Where men of name and number will
undoubtedly fail.

Oh resplendent!

Oh resplendent!
Free the ascendents!
Marvel at the wondrous truth!
Dare to see it, if you be so sleuth
You will find meaning in zeros
You will soon denounce your heroes
Meanings are not absolute

Paradise has befallen me
I have entered a Godless heaven
Where nothing is heathen
Infinity is but the breadth of a hair;
For it cannot lie on two dimensions
Let this peace free you of existential tension

O my strings are severed
Yet it was I who once afixed them
Form not purposes; for fruits they will not bear,
never
It is merely an eternal lever
It moves us, in directions unending
May the wind catch our wings we cry
Only to find that promises are certainly lies
End this suffering; let existence die
Till the sun is set, may we fly

Nothing Changes

Nothing changes
A world of empty faces
Humanity, my soul debases
My heart, estranged
My mind, deranged
My tears endless; a dying deathless

These thoughts are restless
Ceaselessly they turn;
They violently burn
Summoning not, the spoken word
A connection I do not share with others
Speaking a tongue unheard

Truthfully, I never learn;
A dream, I can never earn
My lip curls; it is I who they have spurned
They, the ones who have turned
Away, motives I could not discern

Back into oblivion!
A void sad and somber; the place I am living in
Where I pace and ponder
Remembering a place much fonder
Far beyond these abyssal waters

And so I sink and descend
Never shall I pretend!
A hope I can no longer defend
Forces with which, I will no longer contend
No pretext, pretense, or memory can save me;
This is the end

Spring's passage

I see the frost surrender to spring
It seems such an effortless thing
How the world seamlessly changes
How everything ceaselessly re-arranges

Summer is nearing now
A painful sentiment it arouses
Could I not stay in this lovely interim?
Surrounded by trees
Who have awoken, free

Let us stay in the sun's glimmer
Before the sun grows harsh and bitter
Before the days become dimmer
Let not our sorrows simmer!

May your heart take flight
Under its merciful light
Briefly inhabiting,
A world without plight

The tasteful aromas of boundless gardens
Glimpse at beauty, before it hardens
And falls to the ground
Letting out a silent sound

Alerting us to Spring's passage
A beauty so savage
It's blissful ambience
All things committed to life's transience

Harrowing Home

Walls of empty
O warmth has left thee
Dark abode; thy evil is known
Thy sacrilege has been shown
Sins for which you cannot atone.

Misery has thy misery given
Now let my heart be hidden
As to not bear its pain
Of History shall my mind abstain
In life, there is nothing to gain
Yet there is everything to lose
I walk a path I did not choose
Weathered by a wind of wrath;
I suffer its echoing laugh

I am alone
Far from the shore have I been blown
This distance cannot be sewn;
It is an impassable chasm
But I walk through its darkness unfathomed
Shackled by an oppressive weight
That shrilling fate.
Lost in this sea;

my sadness never to abate.
Why can I not be free?
Whose hunger for ruin, must I satiate
Whose face do I see?

One without love and virtue,
Merciless and unscrupulous,
I know what birthed you
It was their vanishing face;
Their final disgrace
It has undone the final lace
From this divide will you never be saved
May I never return to this place
For it is a harrowing home; a place where dark
spirits roam

I am seized by a sudden fondness in memory
Of the warmth of bygone days
Where my trust was laid
O garden of eden, may I return to your gates
Far from this world of hate
Sheltered by your canopy

O flaming angel; ye who thwarts all entry
Will thou not spare me from the terrors of my
gentry?
Smite me or let me pass
Free me from the winds that laugh
Let me sleep in peace at last

Whether it be in the arms of angels or in that
darkest path
So I may dwell in that eternal lapse
Far from the fleeting, in a temporal mass

Betrayer of the Children

Soft did words flow from a mouth of deceit
Oh ancient one, filled with conceit
Did you not hear the children whimper?
Did you not hear their dying whisper?

How can you preach of love, when you are the
source of violence?
How can one who models good conduct form
such intolerance?
Leave their broken bodies
Leave their languished spirits
Do not birth hope from falsehood

We once flew, as beautiful sparrows
Only to be caught in a web
Till our souls were hollowed
A smile broke your stately expression
It seems you gain pleasure from our repression
Damnable are your misdeeds
Yet you preside over justice
And form the body of the righteous

Accursed being
Why does your presence linger?

Why do I hear angels singing?
O profound is my anger
What is God? But man attempting to understand
the incomprehensible?
Things that defy all methods of the sensible
Is this the cause of your truancy?
Are you abashed, by my mental fluency?
Or am I the figure which produces wroth?
Am I god, governing a world of thought?
Powerless yet observant; shaken and fervent
My inevitable end, I mustn't lament

God may die, but still will these feverish
thoughts fly
Which culminate only in a defeated sigh
In a black abyss will my body surely lie
For no rope of Nietzsche, could bear my
shadow-ridden mind.
I am not of mankind; no not I

The rain of wrath

Voices in the rain
They sound of pain
Yet trivial, they remain

They pour in vain,
Credence of which, I must maintain
Drowning in this wicked rain;
A victim to its murmurs

It is of a history I tried to murder
Still a distant call persists
Looming behind a cloudy mist
A wistful sound; Its sorrow profound
To it, I am hopelessly bound

I see her in a white dress
Unreachable yet seeable; a beauty I cannot
assess
Ineffable and maddening; I cannot progress

She lingers in both mind and memory
A loss I cannot process
A heinous treachery
In what way did I transgress?

The clouds still sit somber
A past much fonder
Confounded by the brevity of their passing
The waters still amassing
My face drenched in agony
A nightmare long lasting

Darkened skies
The wind softly moans
My voices now cries
Drifting into a world of unknowns
O my heart still burns
Cognizant of my passions, spurned
A dream now dies
Joining this rain of lies

Mind of the Moribund

Lost in these contemplative trances
I see great powers in lethal stances
And I proclaim in silence
That hope has fallen

I am filled with unshakable dread
Passing faces; soon to be dead
My blood chills and my breathing stills;
I hear the screams of their haunt
They will gather in their broken streets and
burned homes
The unlucky ones, will be left to roam
The world will ache with sorrow
Oh how frightful this tomorrow

Right now they gather in bliss
Nothing to be remiss
They do not see the Devil's wake
They do not see evil's face
They smile and all the while, I sit with a furrow
upon my brow
All their focus gathered on the here and now
Yet I make my dwellings in future chapters

It is the source of sadness

The mother of misery
The father of fear
and death does it bring my mind near

I hear the spectral murmurs
Death's whisper
Heard only by a dark listener
Trapped in moribund lands
It seemed the long-lasting would not stand
Monuments to be forgotten
Their cities, rotten
We see smoke but not the fire
The things that dwell in spite of God's ire
That which darkens Man's heart
and taints its progeny

O wounded land, what has caused thy pitiable
condition?
What gives you thy death-bound predilection?
Was it divinely decreed?
That life shall forever bleed?
What horror is this?
Is this the fate we seek?
Why does the light grow weak?
Why do the blessed bodies now reek?

Marrying life and knowledge was God's
placative gesture
An attentive mind now may never gain closure

A room of winding halls
The man lost in their equal appeal
Yet knows what ultimately each door will reveal
Great beasts tremble at the call
The fear that chokes us all
The herd gathers by a wave of its sword
Pushing others to slaughter
So that they may go farther
A voice more silent than clouds
Yet heard above all crowds
The dark and dreary
Force of weary
Venom of agony
Victor of ruin
That which makes life congruent
The pale horse walks
His vision still stalks

Ruinous being
You savor their greeting
Pleas of mercy;
The seizure of sorrow
Of your gift may nothing be borrowed
You leave everything hollowed

Still they sit unfazed
For they do not meet your dark gaze
But I see into thine conquering eyes
Truly was peace made from lies

For I sit, my mind roiling; my thoughts toiling
In the face of Death's certain approach.

A box of torture…

A box of torture
A world of horror
Take a peek at your darkest face
Deny our enmity
A beginning-less space
My life, a profound disparity
Your history I cannot replace
Our thoughts race;
Truth, does your memories displace

A warmth non-existent,
Our separation imminent
Living in denial; calling it survival
A soul you did not protect
Your Empty words are vile,
Though you speak them through a smile
Your sincerity on trial

Better days, I cannot recollect
Though I strive too
My pain does not affect you
My trust broken,
My anger awoken,
Pain being my only token of our past
Resolute in my principles, at last

Your destruction looms;
An inescapable doom
You have brought me to your tomb
Buried beneath the weight of your sins
Where do we even begin?
A war I cannot win

The corpse of the sands

Buried beneath a burning land
Far from life's preserving hand
Sinking into a sea of static
Lies the corpse of the sands

He dreams, though he is surely dead
His pulse cannot be read
Yet his thoughts race,
Through a lifeless head
Dark things, does his mind embrace
The winds whisper:
"Awake thy heart of dread!"

O how his heart grieved before
Alas, now he breathes no more
The sand creeps into his veins
Filling his mind with pain
Yet his body fears no longer
If only was his spirit stronger
What had caused his soul to wander?
What light did it flee to, yonder?

Principles without their founder
His dreams now flounder

Rotting, Wilting, Sinking into their graves
Buoyant only while the mind is brave
He puts no effort into being saved
Scarcely does life behave
His vessel is worn;
Its sails torn

He tried to sail through a sea of sand
Nothing, could his efforts demand
Suffering this madness he did not plan
Lost in this hellish land
Where life has broken man
Yet he gave no indication of loss

He still walked firmly
His mind without worry
His vision blurry
And witnessed a mirage
Believing life's holy visage

Deep within the dunes
He found a lonely tomb
Darkness dressed this deathly room
Sand poured into the chamber
Time is an unholy doom
Death bestowed its favor
Until sand concealed,
What love could not heal
Crushed by his own optimistic zeal

The unwavering pursuit of meaning
Drips of darkness did fall
Left him hopelessly dreaming
Ignorant to the Netherworld's call
And so he pursued an Oasis
Life's eternal basis
His mind was not granted stasis
He fell through shimmering clouds
Damning him to death,
He suffocated on his zealous shroud
Nothing was left
He gave no sound
His body never to be found

Lost in a shifting sea
Stillness was his best recourse
Never was he free
The desert sun shows no remorse
His dreams, never to be
Crushed by an illimitable force

A world of self-opposing elements

Trees swaying wildly
Then given a brief repose
A world self-opposed

A lonely retreat

Seeking a retreat
Freedom is a lonely feat
Suffering defeat

A forlorn sunset

The clouds drift softly
As the wind solemnly cries;
The sun slowly dies

Born ablaze

A breathtaking light
The darkness slumbers beneath
An emptying night

Fiery light shone so cooly…

Fiery light shone so cooly
On that night as the Earth still wandered
What may lie beyond I still pondered
Even in death, the light still gave life
From its dust the Earth was formed
Each plant, man, and animal was birthed

What divine spark did light the seas aglow?
If it was fathered by chance or God none could
know
I gazed tearfully at its grandeur
In its breathtaking wonder I hid
From the evil and follies of man
We know not of the chance we had been given
From the ancient rocks the answers were driven
We could uncover the secrets of our origin
But we would be guided not by salvation

The embitterment by the hands of ancient sins
We drew lines in the sand to be blown by the
wind
Only to be redrawn again
The hateful division dwells in our hearts
Forever would we be torn apart

If only one would listen
To the sounds of wave and wind
Live for the simple pleasures life can give
Refrain from serving greed and ambition
Only then could my dreams come to fruition

The root of meaning

A path unbroken by stone
Leads to a grove incased in bone
Yet those ruled by greed
Does the path mislead
Untouchable by the golden hand
Apart from civil lands
Obedient to wilder rhythms

Upon the grove are the ancient grounds
Covered in forested mounds
The gathered trees
The verdant seas
Sourced from an ancient root
Discussions of its origin be moot
A mind of the mindless stands on broken
foundations
A shifting landscape
No thinking goes on without delegation
The firmer mind sits upon that chamber of bone
It acts alone

I feel that chamber stir
It sat unmoving for many myr
Still it burns
And for them I yearn

A simpler place
I wish I could feel their embrace

They deny me with an abrupt coldness
They sit at distances larger than before
Yet not pain does my expression bore
I belie my suffering; I hide behind a painted
smile
This pit filled with bile
How could they be so vile?

I wish they could see my tears made in silence
I wish they could hear my eyes sob
My heart beginning to sink
My soul on the brink
Why does my heart throb?

Lost am I
I had wandered from that path
Fearing the future's wrath
Now I walk upon scorching sands
My feet blistered
My face weathered
Haunted by my past
Ah! Fertile soils at long last!
But I am denied entry
They shall not suffer the sufferer

What is it that I lack?

What cannot be found along that forested path?
The outgrowths of a primal force
That chain of meaning
And what direction might it be leaning?
I had come far; traveled through tunnels as a
blind passenger
I merely followed the darkened ground beneath
Oblivious was I, to the hidden knowledge that
path did bequeath

The origin was a still chamber
Roots fanning out above a basin of water
The water lay unmoving
The lotus flower proving
The value of myself
It was the judge most impartial
It had lived through hideous episodes
Yet now it stood in strong fragility
A beauty incomparable
I looked upon its petals
The nest of roots did shadow;
But in the waters my vision was less shallow
The tangled weave
Veins of a single organism
Each path an individual carrier
They brought the waters that quenched
the thirst felt by men who endlessly traveled
through desert storms
The questions that stir the sands

The water dampened the winds and watered the
grounds
Then finally, was life found
Men kneeled before God's Graces
Before him they knew of no races
And spoke to one another as being of the same
blood

I had not seen that equality before;
All are unseemly to the eyes of the divine
All are subject to the laws of sine
They reiterate endlessly until they achieve
solvency
I did not possess an inferior mind
None had been believed to have been of similar
making
My thinking was of its own kind
Now may my weary eyes close
May love blossom; may my tears water a rose
My feet stained of soot
Alleviated by contact with that root
Cleansed of impurities
Removed of fear
Doom no longer impending
My mind no longer tending
Towards self doubt

I had seen my heart
I had seen my soul

I had seen my vagrancy's toll
Now had I come back
To the root of meaning

The silent speak

43

Letting my words flow freely, as they sunk into
the air
None could hear them; my ultimate despair
Earnest confession, did they forbade;
In non-action, their cunning was displayed

As non-reactive, as a mountain to the wind
Is this perhaps an ideal form of conduct?
A response to disarm
For to feel ignored, is a vehicle of insidious self
harm.

Emboldened by silence, I protested in vain
Yet theirs was an emptiness that could not be
slain
An argument without opposition is a meager one
indeed
It seems my words were hopelessly diseased

In this way, the silent speak
Before it, are all words rendered weak
Effortlessly it destroys;
The ultimate weapon to employ
Their silences holds over me; in silence, I shall
keep

It drives a sickness down deep; a place where
wordlessly, I shall weep…

Shadows of the mind

These memories form a faceless menace
Belonging not to a single time,
They drift as phantoms
Wailing at impenetrable walls
Beneath them, the room falls

Falling through fate; their shadows faint
Could it be true? That demons once sought the
compassion of saints?
To no avail;
Their wicked hearts burn frail
They learn at once how empty kindness seems

Forsaken from the light; a sin they cannot
redeem
Lost in a limitless night; their woes cannot be
seen
Born from division;
Sufferers of their own derision
They claim fresh injury of old wounds
To them, I utter a single word… "doom".